The Earth

The Earth is a huge ball that spins round and round in space. Its surface is covered by water and land. If you could look down at the Earth from up in space, you would see lots of clouds swirling over its surface. Through the clouds you would see the blue colour of the oceans and seas. Nearly two-thirds of the Earth is covered with water. A layer of air, called the atmosphere, surrounds the Earth.

Sun's rays

North Pole

daytime

Equator

night time

axis

South Pole

Day and night

The Earth takes 24 hours to turn all the way round – that is one day and one night. When your country is facing the Sun, it is daytime for you. But as the Earth turns you away from the Sun, everything around you grows darker. During the darkness of the night, your country faces away from the Sun. When you wake up and everything is light again, this is a new day.

△ The Earth always spins around an imaginary line through its middle that we call the Earth's axis. The axis runs through the North and South Poles. Right around the middle of the Earth on the outside is another imaginary line, called the Equator.

5

Our world

From space, the Earth's surface looks smooth – but it isn't really. It has hills and valleys and mountains and gorges, even under the sea. This map is flat, but it shows the most important features on the Earth's surface.

▷ All the land in the world is divided up into seven big areas called "continents". They are Africa, Asia, Antarctica, Europe, North America, Oceania and South America. The continents are shown in different colours on the map.

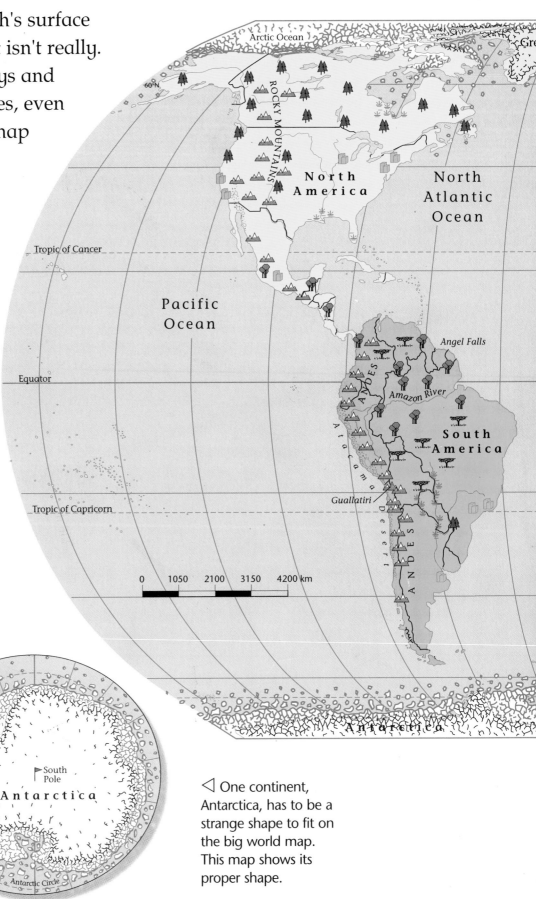

Arctic Ocean

Gre

60° N

ROCKY MOUNTAINS

North America

North Atlantic Ocean

Tropic of Cancer

Pacific Ocean

Equator

Angel Falls

A N D E S

Amazon River

Atacama Desert

South America

Tropic of Capricorn

Guallatiri

A N D E S

0   1050   2100   3150   4200 km

Antarctica

South Pole

Antarctica

Antarctic Circle

◁ One continent, Antarctica, has to be a strange shape to fit on the big world map. This map shows its proper shape.

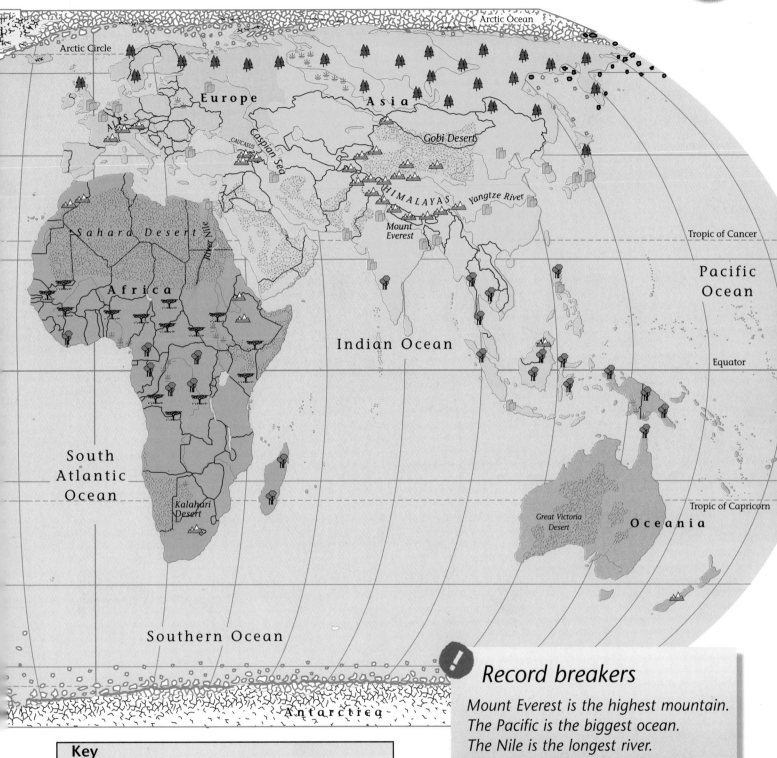

Arctic Ocean

Arctic Circle

Europe

Asia

ALPS

CAUCASUS

Caspian Sea

Gobi Desert

Sahara Desert

River Nile

HIMALAYAS

Yangtze River

Mount Everest

Tropic of Cancer

Africa

Pacific Ocean

Indian Ocean

Equator

South Atlantic Ocean

Kalahari Desert

Great Victoria Desert

Tropic of Capricorn

Oceania

Southern Ocean

Antarctica

Key

desert		high mountains	
marsh		cold forest	
ice on land		savannah	
ice on the sea		hot forest	
country boundary		very large cities	

! Record breakers

Mount Everest is the highest mountain.
The Pacific is the biggest ocean.
The Nile is the longest river.
The Caspian Sea is the biggest lake.
Angel Falls is the highest waterfall.
Guallatiri is the highest volcano.
Greenland is the largest island.
The Sahara is the biggest desert.

7

Sky above, Earth below

We live on the outside part of the Earth. Around and above us is the air we breathe. Beneath us is the Earth's crust, or outer layer. The crust is made of hard rocks, which have been wrinkled and bent to make mountains and valleys.

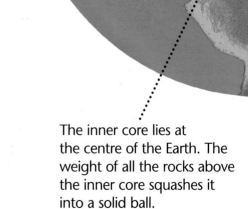

The crust is the Earth's outer layer. It is much thinner than the other layers.

Under the crust lies the mantle. The rocks in the mantle are red-hot, and some of them are so soft that they ooze about.

The rocks in the outer core are so hot that they have melted into a liquid.

The inner core lies at the centre of the Earth. The weight of all the rocks above the inner core squashes it into a solid ball.

To the centre of the Earth

Can you dig right down to the centre of the Earth? If you tried, you would soon find it getting much too hot. As you go deeper, the rocks become hotter – and hotter! Scientists think that the very middle of the Earth is 60 times hotter than boiling water.

A blanket of air

The Earth is wrapped up in an invisible layer of air called the atmosphere. Without this air, there would be no living things on Earth. The atmosphere acts like a blanket. It keeps us warm by trapping the heat of the Sun. And the air in the atmosphere contains important gases such as oxygen, which we breathe to keep us alive. The atmosphere also acts like sunglasses. It stops some of the Sun's harmful rays from reaching the ground.

satellite

Space Shuttle

gas balloon

hot-air balloon

aeroplane

△ We cannot explore deep inside the Earth, but we can travel up into the atmosphere, in balloons and aircraft.

◁ The atmosphere has several different layers. Higher up, the air gets thinner and colder, and there is less oxygen to breathe. In the very highest layers there is hardly any air at all.

The moving Earth

Imagine what it would be like if the ground beneath your feet suddenly started to move! This is what happens during an earthquake. The top layer of the Earth bends and shakes. When a volcano erupts, it can be even more dramatic. Melted rock from under the surface bursts out through a crack in the Earth's crust in a red hot stream.

Volcanoes

Deep under the Earth's surface are pockets of hot, melted rock. If there is a crack in the surface, this hot rock forces its way up and out of the crack. Tonnes of fiery, melted rock called "lava" blast out of the crack. As the lava flows away from the crack, it cools down and hardens into new rock. This new rock piles up around the crack to form a volcano.

▽ An erupting volcano is a terrifying sight. Lava bursts out from the top, and enormous clouds of ash and steam choke the air. Sometimes, a volcano can even explode and be completely blown apart.

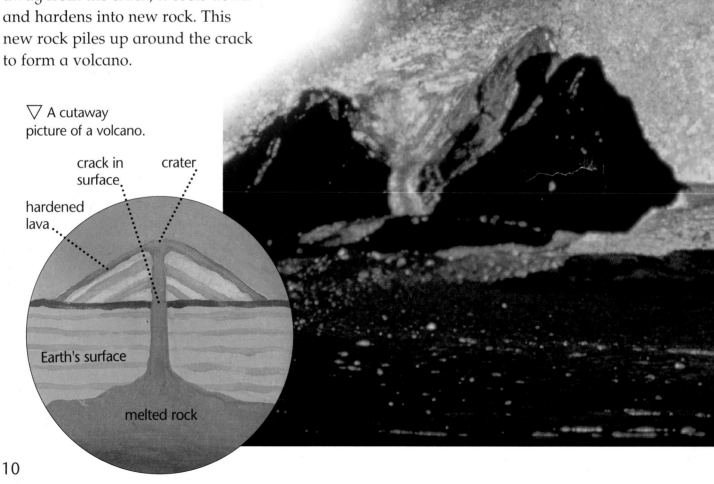

▽ A cutaway picture of a volcano.

crack in surface

crater

hardened lava

Earth's surface

melted rock

Earthquakes

When the Earth starts to shake violently, huge cracks open up in the Earth's surface.

Buildings fall down and roads split apart. Bridges break in two and trees are ripped out of the ground. The land tilts and sends loose rock sliding downhill. Earthquakes under the sea can cause enormous waves that race to the shore and flood the land. These giant waves are called tsunamis.

The biggest bang

Over 100 years ago, in 1883, a volcanic island in Indonesia blew up. It was called Krakatau. The explosion of Krakatau made one of the loudest bangs ever. People heard it over 4800 kilometres away! A huge cloud of ash blotted out the sun for two whole days.

△ A volcano may not erupt for many years, or it may stop erupting altogether. Thousands of years ago, this lake was part of a huge volcano. But the volcano stopped erupting, and now the crater where lava once poured out has filled with water.

Shaping the landscape

We think of a mountain as something big and solid, and it always looks exactly the same. Yet a mountain is changing every day. Wind, cold and water are wearing it away, cutting and carving the rock into new shapes. All around us, the landscape is slowly changing. The land is always being worn away somewhere. At the same time, new land is being made somewhere else.

Wearing away rocks

The weather can break down rocks in different ways. Water pours into cracks in the rock and freezes. The ice splits off small pieces of rock. Rivers cut away the land to make valleys and gorges. In hot dry places, the wind blows sand that scrapes away at rocks – just like sandpaper. And the sea's waves pull up pebbles and throw them at the cliffs, wearing away more rocks.

rain and ice wear away mountains

river carries away pieces of rock

cliffs are worn away by the sea

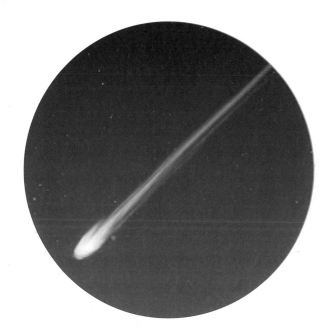

Shooting stars

Have you ever seen a sudden streak of light in the sky? It was probably a shooting star. Shooting stars are not stars at all. Lots of small pieces of rock are flying around the Solar System. Some of them rush straight towards the Earth. When they reach the atmosphere, the rocks become very hot and burn up. This burning is what you see in the sky.

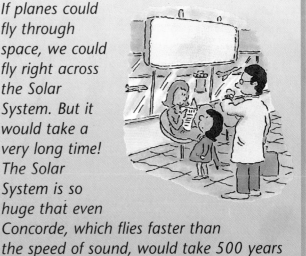

❗ Amazing space!

If planes could fly through space, we could fly right across the Solar System. But it would take a very long time! The Solar System is so huge that even Concorde, which flies faster than the speed of sound, would take 500 years to fly right across!

▽ Saturn has rings around it. These are made of lots of separate pieces of ice.

▽ Uranus also has rings. It was the first planet to be discovered by someone using a telescope.

▽ Neptune is so far from the Sun that it takes 165 years to go right round. It has a ring, too.

▽ Pluto is on the edge of the Solar System. It was only discovered about 70 years ago.

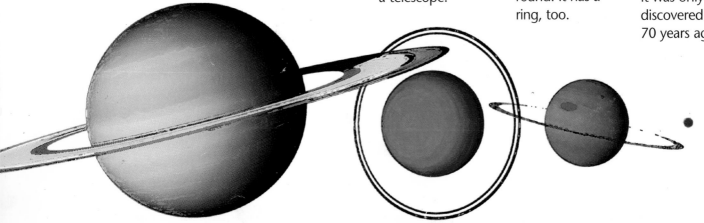

The stars

Have you ever tried counting the stars? It is a very difficult thing to do. There are thousands of them! Even if you could count all the stars you can see, there are millions more that you cannot see without a telescope. Every one of these stars is a glowing ball of gas, just like our Sun.

△ This cloud of gas out in space is called the Orion Nebula. One day in the future, it may become a star.

How a star is made

Where do stars come from? Out in space, there are clouds of dust and gas between the stars. As these clouds move along, they pull more dust and gas towards them. The gas is crushed tightly into a ball, and becomes very, very hot. The star is a bit like a giant power station, giving out lots of heat and light.

The Milky Way

Stars are not scattered evenly through space. They come together in enormous star groups, called galaxies. Our Sun is part of a galaxy called the Milky Way. You can easily see the Milky Way on a clear night. It stretches in a misty band right across the sky.

Shapes in the sky

If you look carefully, you can see that some bright stars make shapes in the sky. The shapes can look like animals, or like people. They have names too. There is a Great Bear and a Little Bear, a Dragon, a Scorpion and a Dog.

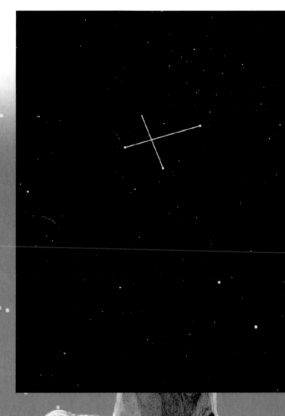

▽ If you live in the northern half of the world, one of the easiest star shapes to see is Orion the Hunter. You can find it by spotting three bright stars in a row – these are Orion's belt. (You can only see Orion in the winter.)

▷ If you live in the southern half of the world, you will always be able to see the Southern Cross in the night sky. Its four bright stars make the shape of a cross.

Why do stars twinkle?

When you look at a star in the sky, it seems to twinkle. In fact, the star is giving out steady beams of light. This light has to travel a very long way through space to reach us. Then it has to pass through the Earth's atmosphere, the layer of moving air that surounds our planet. The air bends and breaks up the star's beams of light - and that makes the light twinkle.

Exploring space

The Universe is a very mysterious place. We have started to explore just our own tiny corner of it. Spacecraft with people on board have landed on the Moon. Other people have spent many weeks inside space stations going round the Earth. Spacecraft with nobody on board have travelled much farther – right to the edge of the Solar System.

△ Most spacecraft are used only once. But the Space Shuttle can be used again and again. When it takes off, the Shuttle has a huge fuel tank and two rocket boosters attached to it. When the fuel runs out, these break away and fall back to Earth.

△ We can look at space through telescopes. But the dust and winds in the Earth's atmosphere get in the way. In 1990, scientists sent a telescope up into space to get a clearer look. It is called the Hubble Space Telescope. It sends us amazing pictures of faraway stars and galaxies.

Walking in space

Astronauts sometimes have to work outside their spacecraft. They wear a special suit with its own supply of oxygen so they can breathe. The backpack is really a tiny jet engine. The astronauts use it to move around outside the spacecraft.

Glossary

Antarctic the area around the South Pole.

Arctic the area around the North Pole.

astronaut a person who flies in a spacecraft.

atmosphere the layer of air that surrounds the Earth.

axis a straight line around which something turns.

ceramic a material like pottery, which is made from clay that has been baked until it is hard.

climate the kind of weather that a particular area usually has.

desert an area where hardly any rain falls. Few animals and plants can live there, because it is so dry.

Equator an imaginary line right around the middle of the Earth. The hottest places in the world are near the Equator.

fossil the remains of a plant or animal from long ago. Many fossils are found inside rocks.

fuel something that is used up to produce energy, for example by burning it.

galaxy a group of millions of stars. Our Sun is in a galaxy called the Milky Way.

gravity the force that pulls objects towards the Earth.

hurricane a violent storm with heavy rain and very strong winds.

lava rock that is so hot, it is liquid. Volcanoes often spout lava when they erupt.

mineral a type of substance found in the ground, such as oil or coal.

ore a rock which is rich in one type of metal.

oxygen a gas in the air, which we need to breathe to stay alive.

planet a huge ball of rock or gas or ice that goes round and round the Sun. The Earth is a planet, and so are Mercury and Saturn.

Poles the North Pole and the South Pole. The Poles are at opposite ends of the Earth's axis. Both places are very cold, but the South Pole is coldest.

rocket a flying machine that is pushed along by a jet of hot gases. Rockets can fly in space because their engines do not need air to work.

satellite an object or a spacecraft that circles around a planet.

seasons the way that the weather changes during the year. Many places have four seasons: spring, summer, autumn and winter.

stars the tiny points of light we see in the sky at night. They are actually enormous balls of very hot gas, but they seem small because they are so far away.

tropics an area of the world close to the Equator. The weather is usually hot in the tropics.

Universe everything we know about, from the Earth, the planets and the Sun to the farthest stars and galaxies in space.

Index